Water For Equity Swap

G. Keith Summers

Copyright © 2016 Author Name

All rights reserved.

ISBN: 978-1532997433
ISBN-13: 1532997434

PROLOGUE

This book is a gift to entrepreneurs and stakeholders within the drought belt of Jamaica's south coast.

It places sustainable community development and sustainable entrepreneurship in a Jamaican context. It drills down to the drought belt and further to a specific parish, St. Elizabeth, then further to a specific resource, water, and even further to the enterprise model for the profitable distribution of water. It also includes the identification of the community nexus, the adhesive that makes the enterprise compatible and synergistic with the communities within the target market of the enterprise. The enterprise target market is identified. Projected Balance Sheet, Income Statement, Cash Flow and value parameters are automatically generated. These are all contained in a financial planning tool included at the end of the book as an imbedded Excel worksheet. It has the capability of unlimited variance analysis. Every key operational and financial input is subject to change by the user within the model while keeping the financial statements and value parameter outputs relevant and accurate in response to the input changes.

This book is a complete business plan and financial model for anyone who is interested in pursuing the opportunity. The enterprise is modular and scalable. It can, with the proper manipulation of data, apply to any parish, development area or community within the drought belt.

Writing the book stems from a compelling personal belief that national development begins at the most basic rung of the production ladder and the identification and improvement of the basic elements of sustainable community development. I believe that the solution lies in entrepreneurial initiative and community commitment. The business plan and financial model provided in the book will hopefully be a substantial enabling tool in carrying this out. Those aspiring to implement the business enterprise offered here should be aware that the mandates for community development, economic development, and agricultural irrigation are all institutionally parceled out to various government agencies. The risk of encroachment is real, however well intentioned your efforts. Collaboration, real and perceived, is a vital requirement.

Readers with a printed version can request the free financial planning tool from the author at gksummers2004@yahoo.com.

CONTENTS

	Acknowledgments	i
1	OVERVIEW	Pg # 6
2	THE TARGET PARISH	Pg # 14
3	THE TARGET MARKET	Pg # 21
4	THE BUSINESS ENTERPRISE ***IRRIGATE!***	Pg # 27
5	RESEARCH SOURCES	Pg # 45

ACKNOWLEDGMENTS

The inspiration for this book stemmed from two focal points, community development and financial analysis. Acknowledgments are extended to two very diverse spheres of influence.

The community development aspect was substantially attributable to my associates and very close friends at the ***Urban Development Corporation*** who taught me quickly and well the value of community integration as an integral element in understanding communities. Unfortunately that feature has been too often overlooked, overstepped and as a result muffled as an institutional strategy.

The financial analysis aspect recognizes all my consulting clients for their unwitting guidance in developing the financial planning model on which the ***Water For Equity Swap*** was constructed. It was their demands, skepticism, and barely masked resistance to the need for financial planning on a long term horizon that prompted me to build a model as user friendly and flexible as possible.

1 OVERVIEW

"Sustainable development is development that meets the needs of the present without compromising the ability of future generations to meet their own needs."
—World Commission on the Environment and Development

An irony in the path of community development is that what makes you great can also make you vulnerable. If the strength of your community is agriculture in that it provides your livelihood, your economics, your reputation, and if for any reason anything threatens to erode that strength then it becomes a point of vulnerability. The vulnerability can be invasive as it affects families, communities and the nation. One way to address that vulnerability is to insert elements of sustainability. Whatever we produce and however we produce it, we must be comfortable that we can continue producing it with a level of confidence that the physical and attitudinal environment making it possible will remain stable or improve. We must be secure in thinking that the future generations will benefit as much as or more than we are benefitting now, or even how we think we should be benefiting. This attitude underpins true sustainability.

As with any successful concept such as sustainability, this requires a critical balance between the foundation elements of social progress, protection of the natural environment, the careful husbanding of natural resources, and steady and increasing levels of economic development along with progressive employment.

Social progress, for example, can only work if increased levels of communication among community members happen and lead to more informed communal decision making or even constructive disagreements. A place to meet is an important component and this exists in most communities in Jamaica. Development Agencies, corporate benefactors, International Donor Agencies, and other contributory organizations have donated generously to ensure community centers are built wherever possible. A convening body or organization such as Community Based Organizations (CBO) and Community Development Councils, are easy to set up and manage thanks to existing legislation. All told, the framework exists. It is maximizing the potential of these that is weak. The managerial ability to use the local organization to drive community development is in short supply within the communities. Many community organizations are idle, dormant or otherwise ineffective as a result of this. One approach is to have the same entities that make the physical centers and the legal organizations possible ensure that a progressive management mechanism is enabled, not just required, and they should take ownership of the continuance of the mechanism.

It is difficult to overemphasize the importance of the internet particularly in rural communities and should be a staple item in every in every initiative undertaken by development agencies within communities.

Protection of the natural environment is a principle accepted by everyone but not always practised even among people qualified and capable to undertake it. Large corporations, especially operators in the extractive industries could take better care in preserving the environment and they can easily afford to. It is not a mild irony that the responsibility for the preservation of a community's environment, within the context of their own sustainable development, falls to a cadre of people never trained in the implications of its value. They are incapable of formulating a comprehensive program to address it, and are devoid of the financial resources to accomplish it. Notwithstanding, preservation of the natural environment inexorably falls to the community residents. It is probably the weakest link in the chain of sustainable development that community members have to deal with.

The careful husbanding of natural resources goes beyond the level of a concept for the community members. It is rooted in reality. It is the natural resources that drive the tourism trade both local and foreign and thus provides much of the opportunities and sustenance for community members. They need no reminder of this, nor do they need education in this respect. In fact they have a greater appreciation for natural resources than most people outside their community. The beaches, the waterfalls, the rivers, the forests and all the other natural local wonders are theirs in the context of sustainable development. Agriculture is also a natural resource in this context. It, more than anything else, provides a predictable source of income and well being. The husbanding of this resource is threatened not by physical erosion or depletion but by demographics. For many reasons, to the younger generation, farming is not a very attractive occupation so ex-migration for more attractive occupations threatens this natural resource.

Steady and increasing levels of economic development along with progressive employment are the final element and probably the most impactful. It expands beyond the borders of the community to the doorstep of capitalism and financial markets. This element cannot happen without outside help. It brings into play another engine of growth which leverages the resources of the community combined with the resources of external capital under the umbrella of sustainable entrepreneurship. Under typical circumstances the proper combination of capital, labor and profit ensures commercial sustainability. However, sustainable entrepreneurship has two responsibilities that broaden its mandate.

The first is that the enterprise must be scalable and modular. It must be expandable in all directions in that it must be able to shrink, grow, or remain unchanged as circumstances dictate. It must be applicable to and replicable in all similar communities. The business case must work in all communities of a similar socio economic structure. The second is that it must provide the glue that makes community members want to work with the enterprise, produce together, and that encourages them to work that much harder in order to make this development last. It is an elusive element that I call the **community's nexus**, the adhesion or connectivity that binds the enterprise to the community.

The concept of discipline as I see it offers a parallel viewpoint. Discipline in my view is the recognition of something of value and the single-minded unswerving drive to grab it. We are not born with discipline but we are born with a talent to recognize something of value. Both the entrepreneur and the community need to recognize what is of common value. Once that is achieved, the nexus begins to form.

Whatever the enterprise is or does, it is inexorably defined by ownership. An individual or group of individuals owns it. It is his capital that is at risk. If the tide of profitability turns against him then he must make a decision to preserve the integrity of his capital. He is not obligated to share his ownership nor is he obligated to keep the enterprise running even after continued operation works to his detriment. The reality is that the community is more vulnerable than the enterprise because capital is mobile. It can migrate. However, the enterprise stands a greater chance of success if the entire community supports the enterprise, not just the residents who receive trickle down benefits by way of direct employment. This type of employment benefit is opportunistic, not permanent nor sustainable. The community does not own the enterprise, nor should it. Group or cooperative ownership is not the answer but the continued and sustainable benefit to the wider community is as important as the traditional commercial requirements of capital, labor and profit. The benefit that touches the entire population is the community's nexus, the element that binds the community and the enterprise in a sustainable relationship.

The identification of this nexus is very important. It must be something that every community member relates to and the commercial enterprise must be prepared to underwrite. The most intrinsic, pervasive and identifiable group within every community is children. Every member of the community either has a child or more than one, or has a relative or friend who has children, or is a grandfather or grandmother to one, or lives beside a family that has children. The presence of children is permanent. Everybody relates to a program that benefits children because everybody relates to children. Children are the best potential source of preserving the resource of agriculture, being the natural beneficiaries of the existing agricultural class. Any business project that wants to enroll the support of community members, whether they are directly employed or not, needs to bring benefits to the space in the community that every resident relates to. This is the glue that makes community development sustainable. Initiatives that endow benefits to children will enroll the support of all community members and by extension the broad based enduring support of the business enterprise.

"A strongly sustainable organization is one in which all of its behaviours and all the behaviours of all other relevant social, economic and biophysical actors, lead to the possibility that human and other life will flourish on the planet forever."
—Upward Antony, <u>Towards an Ontology and Canvas for Strongly Sustainable Business Models: A Systemic Design Science Exploration</u>, 2013

The success of a business is no longer measured only by its financial profitability but also by its impact on society. This is the benchmark of its sustainability. Emerging from this is the concept of the Triple Bottom Line (TBL). Sustainable entrepreneurship must identify, develop, launch and mange economic opportunities in order to achieve social, ecological and economic gains, the three bottom lines. Social gains include a responsibility to operate to the benefit of its employees, stakeholders and the community in which it operates. Ecological gains call on the enterprise to minimize its environmental footprint, reduce waste and conserve energy. Economic gains translate to profitability as this is what provides the sustainability of capital and remains the most measurable of the three. Also important to note is that these three bottom lines do not happen simultaneously. Social and ecological gains will typically lag behind economic gains because it takes time for the economic gains to define the areas of impact.

Opportunities in a vibrant economic environment typically emerge from market imperfections, inadequate provision of goods and services in commercial enterprises, and other imbalances. What set of circumstances opened the door to private security firms, privately owned mail and package delivery services, private environmental consulting firms, and so many others? From the standpoint of the sustainable business solution, the opportunities must be premised on the natural resources and assets of the community and the residents.

2 THE TARGET PARISH

'In St Elizabeth and the wider southern Jamaica, the period between early December and the end of March traditionally brings very little rainfall; but the current drought is said to be the worst since 2010.'
Jamaica Observer Sunday, February 03, 2013

The drought belt is probably identifiable to the reader almost intuitively as the southern parishes of the island. In this book it loosely captures the parishes of St. Catherine, Clarendon, Manchester, St. Elizabeth and Westmoreland. These parishes share the contradictory distinctions of having not only the lowest incidence of rainfall nationally with severe and destructive periodic drought conditions, but comprise approximately 54% of the identified farming acreage in the country. Within this belt there are enterprise opportunities gravitating around the very shortages that define them. Agriculture as an activity is an absolute requirement in the communities within these parishes. It provides individual sustenance and personal wealth creation to the residents, and contributes to national development and exports. Its production must feed a captive audience of the almost three million local Jamaican residents, export as much as possible, and construct its own sustainable development platform.

Water and its efficient distribution are pivotal to the future of the parishes in this section of the country. Rainfall is a primary source of irrigation water. As shown in the map below ***30-year Mean Rainfall Distribution for St. Elizabeth*** there are distinct bands of rainfall activity.

The southernmost tip of the parish has the lowest incidence of rainfall and increases as you go north within the parish. At the lowest incidence the average amount of rainfall ranges between 768 mm and 1,325 mm. The typical amount of rainfall lost to evapotranspiration is approximately 52%. This process is usually described as "the return of moisture to the air through both evaporation from the soil and transpiration by plants". Taking this into account the usable amount drops to between 369 mm and 636mm. Estimates are that the average farm size in St. Elizabeth requires approximately 600mm of water per annum. Accepting these estimates it would follow that rainfall would have to perform at the highest end of the average range to meet these needs. Jamaica's recent trends suggest that rainfall has been well below the average.

The rainfall incidence at the southernmost tip of the parish is significant for another reason.

If you overlay the map titled ***St. Elizabeth Farming Areas*** on the above mentioned mean rainfall distribution map it reveals that the farming areas identified as "Mixed Farm" is substantially clustered in the area of the lowest incidence of rainfall. The farms targeted for this book are in this mixed farm group. To some degree the mixed farm areas spread into the next higher rainfall incidence band. That next higher incidence band experiences rainfall activity between 1,325mm to 1,775mm. Diluted for the evapotranspiration factor this reduces to between 636mm and 852mm. Even in this band, rainfall activity may fall short of needs.

By extension the success of farming, at least in the parish of St. Elizabeth, resides critically in finding and distributing a source of irrigation water supplementary to rainfall.

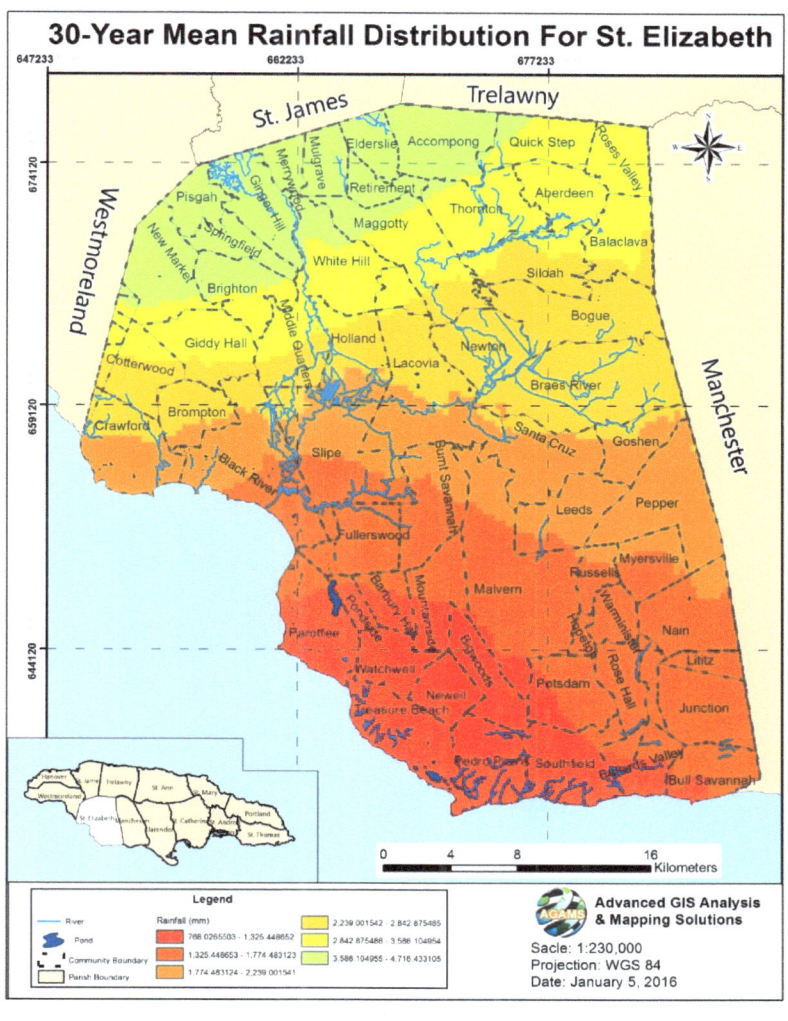

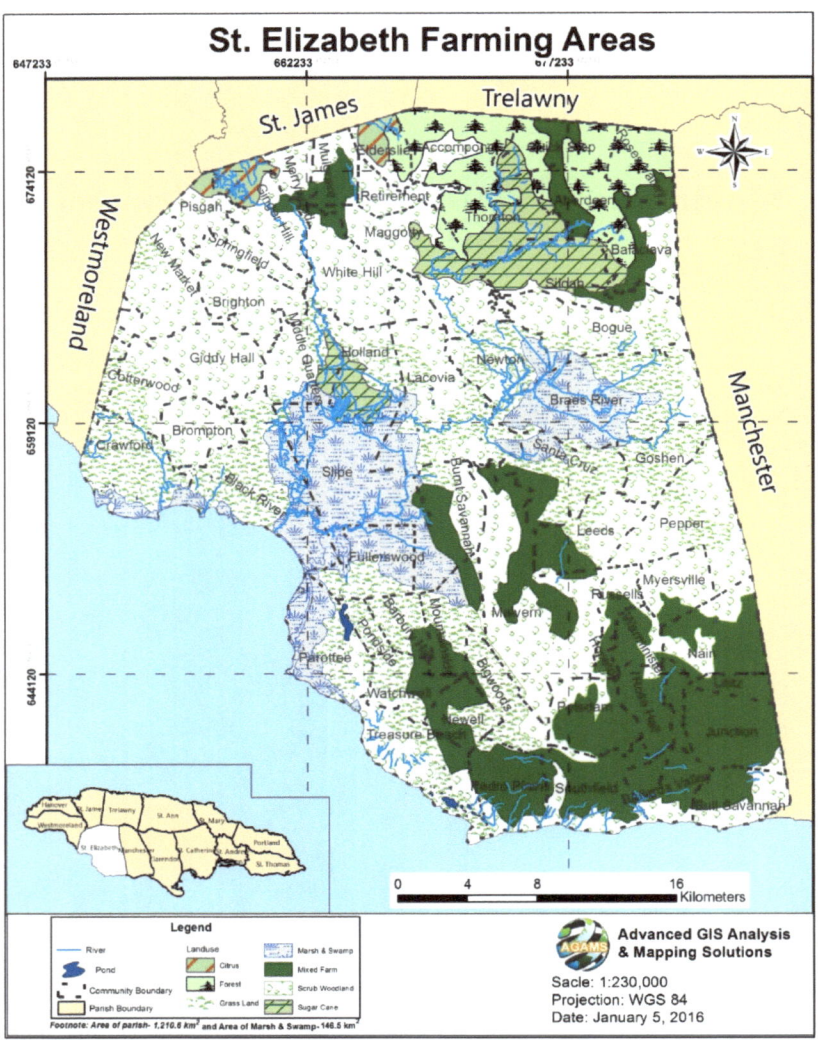

Overlay the map ***St. Elizabeth Well Locations*** on the farming area map illustrated previously. Within the farming areas identified as mixed farming at the southern end of the parish there are 53 wells. This does not account for the wells just outside of the identified areas. Any well in the southern end of the parish, if not located in the mixed farming area is within reasonable trucking distance from that area. The majority of the wells in the parish are owned by large corporations and agencies with a small amount privately owned.

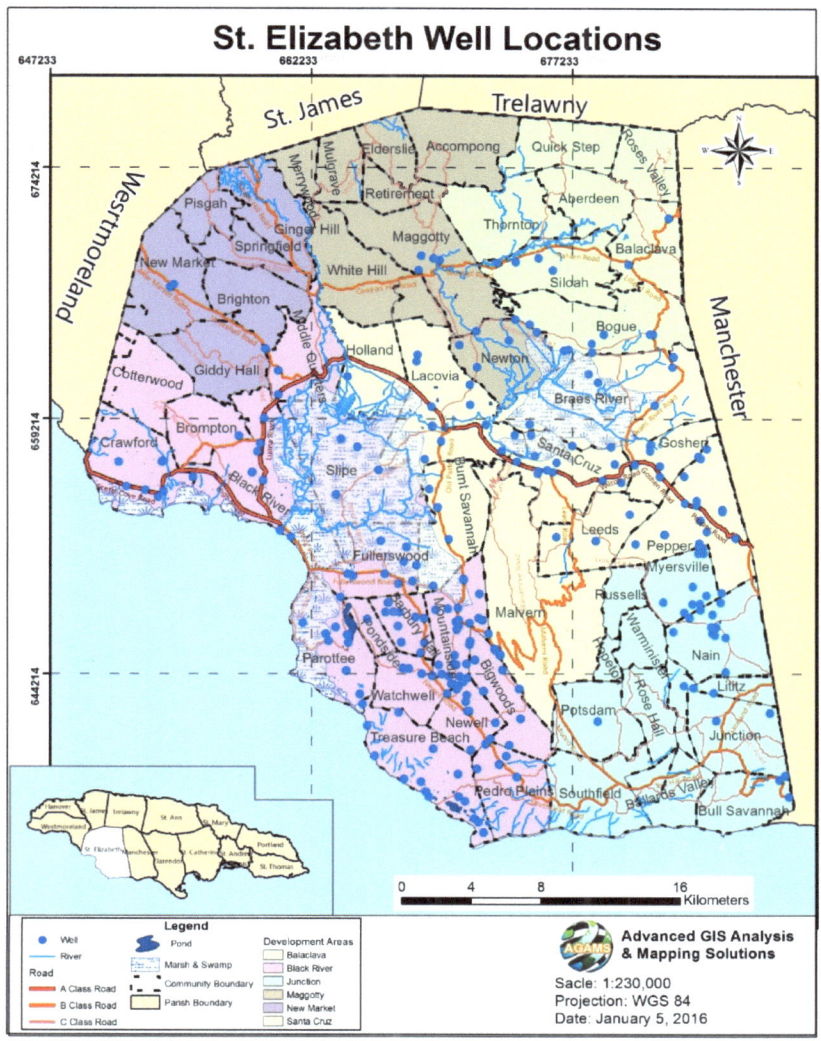

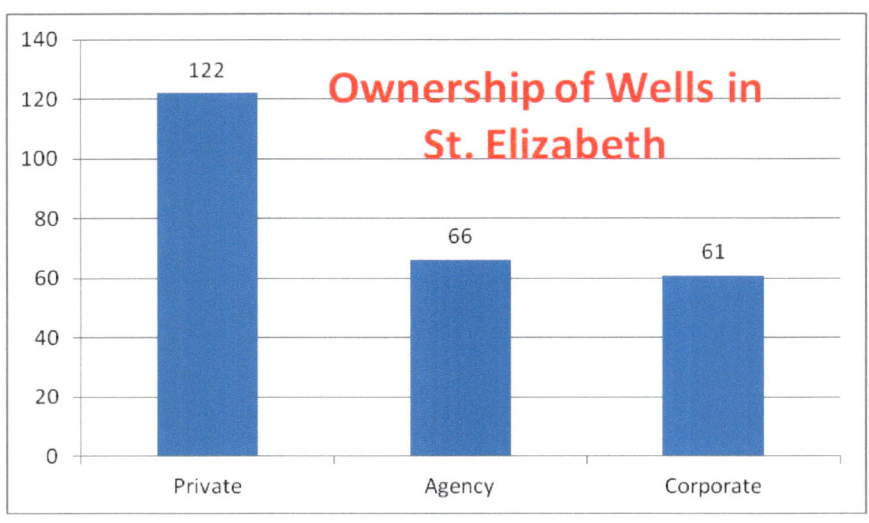

3 THE TARGET MARKET

The majority of farms in Jamaica are small. Those farms in the size category less than one hectare total 151,931 which is 76% of the total amount of farms. If you include farm sizes over one hectare up to five hectares they account for 98% of total farms. Remember that the smaller the farm, the greater are the diseconomies. Access to technology, capital, the best market outlets, all fade as available options as they descend the size scale. These small farms represent a massive constituency of people who need to make their livelihood a sustainable one and all the elements for sustainability do not necessarily reside in their communities. It also represents a huge market to entrepreneurs to develop, implement and operate programs and enterprises that can assist in making sustainable community development happen.

FARMS	Jamaica Total	St. Elizabeth	Clarendon
Gross Farms Reporting	200,540	28,383	27,381
Farms < 1 hectare	151,931	24,628	18,996
	St. Catherine	Manchester	Westmoreland
Gross Farms Reporting	20,177	21,671	17,396
Farms < 1 hectare	14,981	16,657	14,357

The drought belt parishes, for the purpose of this treatment, are St. Elizabeth, Clarendon, St. Catherine, Manchester and Westmoreland. The rest of Jamaica houses 41% of farms less than one hectare in size. The drought belt parishes account for 59%. That is significant. If it reveals nothing else it suggests a fearsome vulnerability to droughts within the agricultural sector in Jamaica. Interpret that observation in the context of people affected and the realization dawns that the segment of people most likely to feel the effects of disastrous drought conditions are the ones least prepared to withstand it, and the ones who stand to lose the most in terms of economic development and personal sustenance. On the other side of the coin a focus on the parishes within the belt in terms of support for economic development will have a disproportionately large impact on this industry sector.

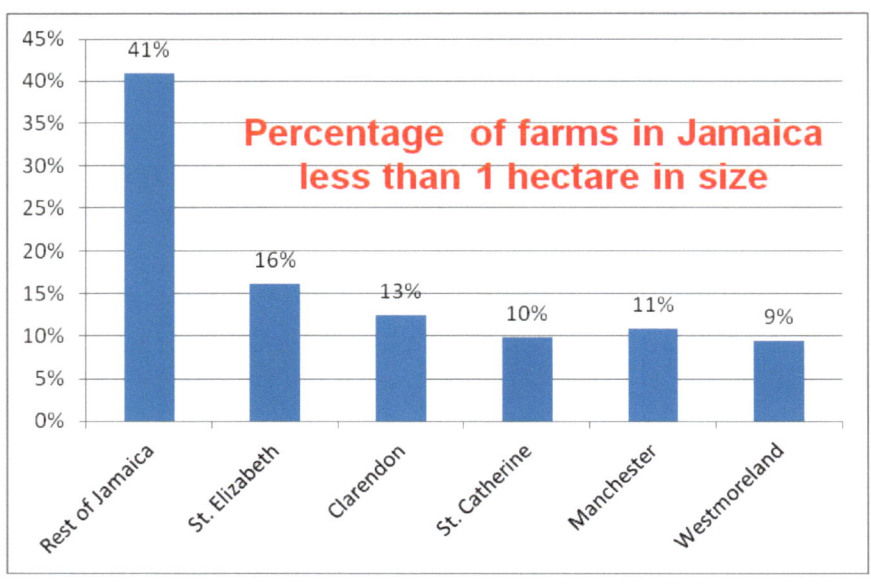

Within this farm size category St. Elizabeth is the largest in terms of total farms followed by Clarendon.

The average farm size is another revealing statistic.

Although the broad size category is less than one hectare, the statistical average size in St. Elizabeth is 0.29 hectares. Only Westmoreland has a smaller average farm size at 0.26 hectares. This effectively defines small farms in the Jamaican context.

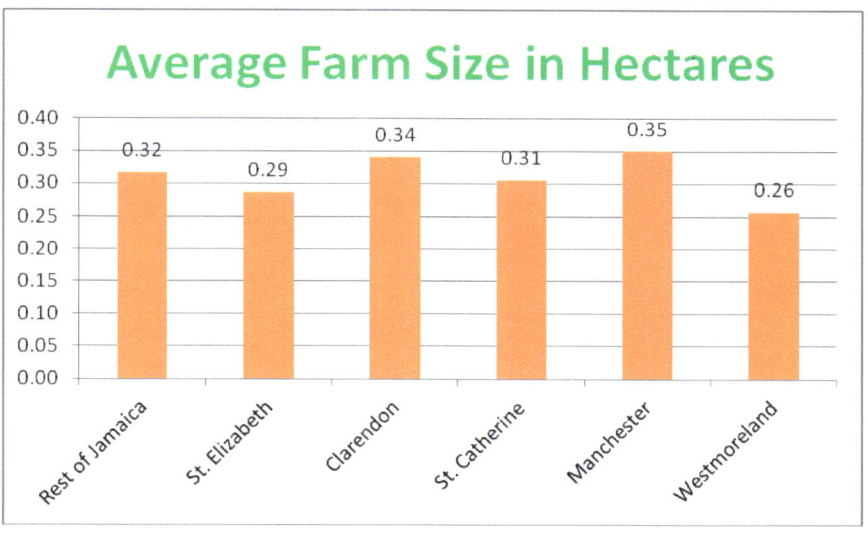

The defining of the target market and its configuration begins here.

The portable irrigation solution is most applicable to certain crops. These are in the category of vegetable, spices, legumes and nuts, roots and tubers, and fruits. Within the drought belt the chart below illustrates how the land is allocated to the various crops.

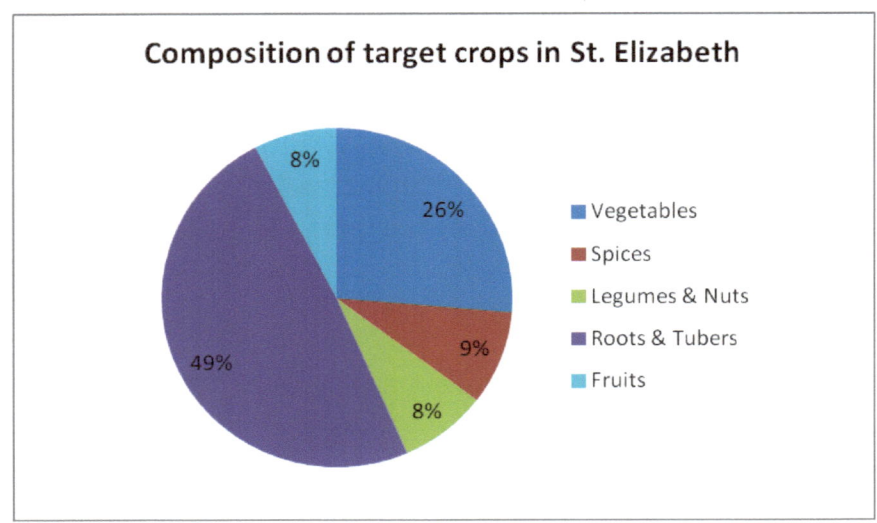

On average, approximately 41% of the agricultural land within this belt grows these crops. The chart below illustrates the percentage of land within each parish allocated to the target crops.

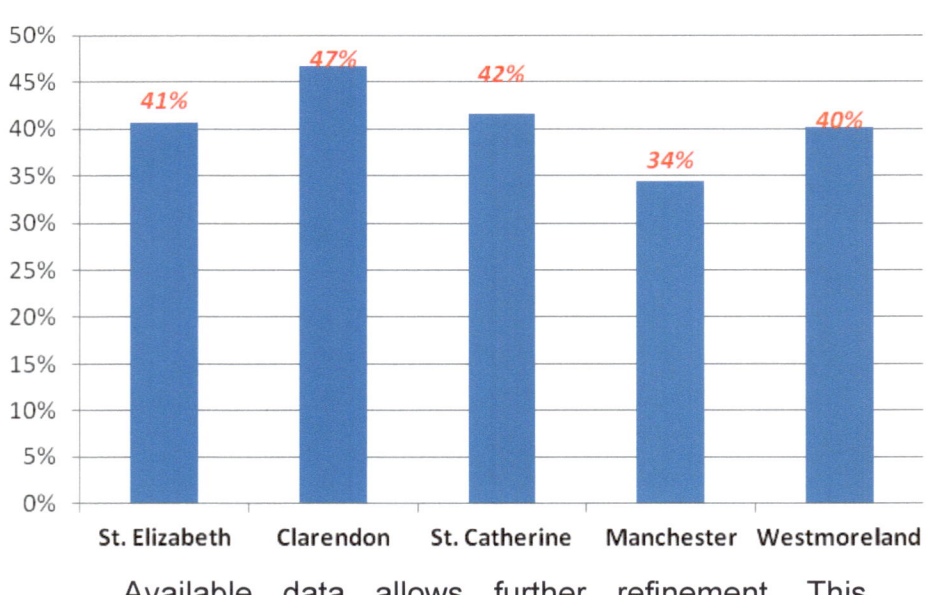

Available data allows further refinement. This

business case calls for sprinklering as the method of water distribution. Within the drought belt parishes there are approximately 36,000 farms under I hectare in size that are appropriately contoured for sprinklering. Only 1,970 currently use this method of distribution. Based on the data at hand the target market is as follows:

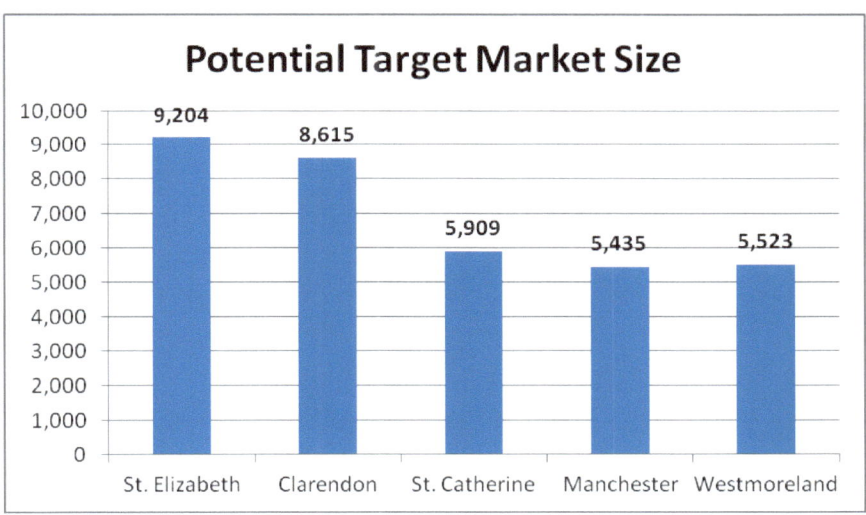

The communities of the parish of St. Elizabeth fall within five Development Areas (DA). The lower southeastern piece of the parish is the Junction DA. The Balaclava DA and Maggotty DA share the opposite end of the map, the northeast corner. The top piece of the north western protruding edge of the parish is the New Market DA. The large Black River DA covers the entire middle of the parish including a piece of the protruding north western tip. If you overlay the Farming Areas Map on the Communities Map it would show that the parts identified as mixed farms are substantially within the southern part of the parish, densely clustered in the Junction DA and then more dispersed within the Black River DA. Otherwise Balaclava DA and Maggotty DA have some clusters of this type of farming. It is within this farming category that the target market resides.

4 THE BUSINESS ENTERPRISE *IRRIGATE!*

IRRIGATE! is a fully portable irrigation solution for small farmers in the rural agricultural belt of Jamaica. It solves the problem of persistent drought conditions that are so destructive to small farmers who rely on rainfall for irrigation. It further addresses the economic development that has eluded these small agricultural communities all over the island.

Rural communities are substantially dependent on agriculture for commercial pursuits, personal sustenance and survival. Water is the lifeblood of this activity. The small farmer in the rural communities of Jamaica, including the drought belt, is substantially dependent on rainfall for irrigation with the next tier of sourcing being commercially delivered water. These sources are the National Water Commission (NWC) and National Irrigation Commission (NIC) or private contractors who source water from these. They are very successful at delivering water to the larger farming sites but there is a niche of small farmers who do not benefit from the activity of these organizations whether for economic or logistical reasons. The target market for the services is primarily those farmers who fall outside the delivery capability of NWC and NIC. However, even those farmers who are currently customers of these two water suppliers will have an interest in the services because the there will be substantial operating and cost advantages. In addition to struggling to afford commercial water there is no efficient distribution system for the water on the farm site. Drip irrigation, a popularly accepted and efficient method of delivery is logistically and economically impractical for many of these farmers. Rainfall, based on data, has been in consistent decline over the recent past, further threatening the economic survival of rural communities. This niche of marginalized farms is the backbone of rural communities and an important component of economic development.

THE WATER SOLUTION

The business proposition is designed to deliver and distribute irrigation water to small farmers (farms less than one hectare in size) profitably, at a price competitive to what currently avails, using a methodology that does not require the farmer to invest in any infrastructure. This will ameliorate the impact of unpredictable rainfall patterns and provide a consistent and reliable source of irrigation. It will further improve the productivity of farms in this category and ultimately the welfare of the residents of small rural communities.

In the Daily Gleaner of Tuesday May 12, 2015:

'The breadbasket Parish of St Elizabeth is currently reeling from the effects of severe drought conditions, with farmers said to be experiencing significant losses as their crops dry up in the field. "Just from the drought alone, many persons would have been losing their

crops because the crops would have received enough sunlight, enough fertiliser, but not enough water to feed the plants through the roots," member of parliament for South West St Elizabeth, Hugh Buchanan told The Gleaner.'

In the same article:

'And, president of the Jamaica Agricultural Society (JAS), Senator Norman Grant, said although the dry conditions have affected the farming community this year, the impact on the sector last year was devastating. In 2014, the agricultural sector suffered losses amounting to $1 billion, with about 18,000 farmers affected. Grant said the drought in 2014 started in April and extended to September. He stressed that it was the worst period of drought that had affected the country in nearly 100 years. Grant said it was too early to predict whether farmers would suffer the same fate this year.'

Again in the Sunday Gleaner January 10, 2016, interestingly in an article entitled **<u>Agriculture to recover from drought by 2016's second quarter - RADA head</u>**:

"Lenworth Fulton, chief executive officer of the Rural Agricultural Development Authority (RADA), is urging farmers still reeling from last year's drought to hold strain as Government continues its assessment and assistance procedures. Fulton told The Sunday Gleaner that preliminary estimates place the loss to the agricultural sector from the drought at some $8 billion, and so far Government has spent approximately $1 billion to assist farmers whose crops would have been significantly impacted.

'People have lost significantly; their whole tomato, Irish potato, yam, and even the drought-tolerant crops. Even last Christmas you wouldn't see the amount of gungo peas that you would want because the crop is definitely late,' Fulton said during an interview at RADA's St Andrew head office.'

The most important component of the success of the enterprise is water.

If water can be delivered efficiently and economically to the target market segment, there is no doubt that production would increase substantially and the well-being of the communities improve. Rainfall is the traditional and in many cases the only source of water. Overland tanker delivery of water, typically sourced from wells is very common but it comes with attendant costs. This operating model was developed to counter the insufficiency and unpredictable nature of rainfall. While it cannot eliminate the cost of water it does eliminate the cash flow burden of purchasing water by making water an equity capital component, requiring it as a capital investment rather than an operating cash flow item. This way the cost of working capital to buy water as needed is eliminated, giving the enterprise a better chance of profitability and success.

In the parish of St. Elizabeth there are about numerous wells. All wells are subject to licensing restrictions as to the use of the water and how much can be extracted. Notwithstanding, this is a large audience from which to secure rights to some of the water. The principle is to approach and present the owner of the well with a business proposal. The proposal is to have him provide water to the program as an equity investment and in return receive an ownership position in the enterprise equivalent to the imputed value of the water over a five year period.

Why would a well owner do this?

A private well owner who has capacity and is appropriately licensed can leverage the available water to own a piece of the enterprise. He uses the water that is still in the ground to own a piece of an enterprise. This takes him one step further to monetizing an asset that has value but at present is substantially dormant and illiquid (in a financial sense) until he eventually uses it or sells it. He is not called on to make any monetary investment, nor is he required to operate the business unless he chooses to negotiate for this right. There may be unknown personal considerations that may provide a multitude of other motivational factors.

National Irrigation Commission (NIC), National Water Commission (NWC), Urban Development Corporation (UDC), Petroleum Corporation of Jamaica (PCJ), National Land Agency (NLA) and many other agencies own and/or control wells. NIC has a core mandate to provide water for irrigation. However it is not structured to deliver water to the small marginal farmer that is the target market of this enterprise. Providing water to the enterprise as a capital investment allows it to expand the reach of its mandate without having to re-equip or expand its operations. Further, it does not cause it to stray from its core mandate. NWC is also a major supplier to the agricultural belt in addition to its mandate to deliver potable water. The ability to expand its reach without re-equipping also applies here. UDC has a development mandate and while it has numerous water sources does not have the responsibility for providing water to farmers that NIC and NWC has. Nonetheless, being an investor here would assist in making development happen, its corporate mantra, without added expense. PCJ has no such mandate to provide water but it does so to selected communities as a part of its corporate community stakeholder responsibility. This enterprise broadens its reach. NLA, similarly, has no such mandate but does own a massive portfolio of properties and is not identified as an owner of any of the St. Elizabeth wells. However, it is conceivable that within its leased portfolio are properties that have wells on them.

Twenty two of the more than forty wells in St. Elizabeth are owned by corporate entities. For the purpose of this discussion they fall in the same category as PCJ, no mandate to provide water, but will do so (if it is not already doing so) to selected communities as a part of its corporate community stakeholder responsibility. These also represent prospective investors.

THE DISTRIBUTION SOLUTION

'In agriculture for instance, sugar cane estates are generally watered by canals, fed from a main source that covers fields of cane through seepage to plant roots. However, that method has been displaced technologically by overhead sprinklers attached to a long rotating boom regulated by computers. I first saw the system in

operation at Appleton sugar estate in St. Elizabeth where several rotating overhead booms, each covering 60 acres, were in use. This operation was very successful in using water efficiency, because two-thirds of the water went directly to the roots of the cane compared to one-third from canals. More sugar for less water!'

<u>**What's up with South St. Catherine reservoir?**</u> **By Edward Seaga**

The Sunday Gleaner July 19, 2015; In Focus page G6

The portable irrigation solution closely resembles what Mr. Seaga describes. It differs only in scale.

The water source in this case can be a river, a storage tank or a water truck. The overhead sprinkler can wet a 150' diameter area and more. The entire system is portable, scalable and modular. This equipment (pump, hoses, and sprinkler head) travels around with the tanker. At the customer location the equipment is positioned and the wetting takes place. On average one tanker can cover four locations per day based on the average farm size in the study.

THE PRINCIPLE OF THE BUSINESS CASE

What is treated here is not just a business model with broad conceptual and philosophical parameters. It is not the cloak or the umbrella that covers the essence of an enterprise or the broad underpinnings to the market. It is the total enterprise in its calculated and calculable detail. It is done this way so that the reader can take the compendium of data and assumptions and use it as if it were his or her own. The reader can modify, adjust, change the data, and apply unlimited variance analysis his own analytical tools using the imbedded Excel worksheet located on the last page of the book. The business is scalable and modular and designed to show profit determinants, both positive and negative for any series or configuration. It is applicable to every parish that relies on agriculture and is divisible into district, community or Development Area pieces.

THE FINANCIAL SOLUTION

The most important financial requirement of the business is profitability.

Identify the section within the parish that is your target market. Estimate the cubic meters (M3) of water your project will require over the next five years to service your target market. Calculate the dollar value of the water for each year based on the market price with a reasonable annual increase in price over the next five years. Discount that five year estimate of dollar values by a rate that adequately recognizes the cost of capital. Calculate the Net Present Value (NPV) of that stream of values. The resulting figure is the true value of the water that the project requires. This is the equivalent capital investment of the well owner.

Dollar Value of water committed over projected period

	Present Values
Year 1	$1,391,681
Year 2	$1,241,023
Year 3	$1,051,714
Year 4	$891,283
Year 5	$755,325
TOTAL	**$5,331,026**

It is the equivalent of investing cash, except that it takes the form of a resource the owner of the well has under his control. As part of the arrangement the well owner must give an enforceable and contractual forward commitment to provide the water necessary to carry out the project.

This contract may be viewed as a distinct and separate intangible asset of the company, subject to amortization although it is not recognized this way in the projections. This forward commitment will have several contractual elements included but key among them is the feature of transferability of the contract. In the event the company fails for whatever reason, the commitment has a distinct and determinable value equivalent to the unused portion of the commitment. In fact, the value is precisely the reverse sequence of the present value stream.

The Net Present Value in dollar terms of the water that is committed entitles the well owner to ownership in the enterprise proportional to the total investment that the project requires. The resulting ownership structure based on the inputs in this version is pictured below.

Original Cash Investment		$7,500,000	58%
Imputed Equity Value of Water		$5,331,026	42%
TOTAL EQUITY		**$12,831,026**	

The use of the original cash investment is to purchase equipment, cover pre-operational costs, and provide working capital on an ongoing basis. These components are subject to change depending on the perspective of the promoter who puts this enterprise together. Any change in these and in fact any change in the imputed equity value of water will change the ownership mix.

Pre-operating costs

Furniture	$549,000
EQUIPMENT -Office	$874,000
EQUIPMENT-Operations	$4,636,000
Rent Deposit	$230,000
TOTAL	$6,289,000

The assumption is that the business promoter will purchase one water truck and rely on water contractors when the capacity of one truck is exceeded. It is assumed that operating and administrative facilities will be established from the ground up. The cash flow summary below illustrates end-of-year position.

CashFlow Summary	Year 1	Year 2	Year 3
Beginning Cash Balance	$0	$11,764,982	$31,462,066
Cash from Operations	$9,130,982	$19,697,084	$25,975,617
Net Cash Used for Investing	($4,866,000)	$0	$0
Net Cash From Financing	$7,500,000	$0	$0
Ending Cash Balance	$11,764,982	$31,462,066	$57,437,683

CashFlow Summary	Year 4	Year 5
Beginning Cash Balance	$57,437,683	$89,504,576
Cash from Operations	$32,066,893	$32,790,032
Net Cash Used for Investing	$0	$0
Net Cash From Financing	$0	$0
Ending Cash Balance	$89,504,576	$122,294,608

The ending cash balance may seem high and may bring into question the need for the size of the initial cash investment. However, it is the early stage cash demands that dictate the level of the cash investment. Looking at the early months' cash balances the justification is clear. Particularly in month 2 the cash balances are dangerously low.

Any cash equity investment less than the amount shown above will result in cash shortfalls in the early months as time is required for the revenue to build to optimum levels. If, for example, the initial cash investment were reduced to $6,500,000 the following early stage cash balances would be as follows:

Early stage cash balances

	Month 1	Month 2	Month 3
Ending Cash Balance	$829,357	($664,091)	($34,227)

	Month 4	Month 5	Month 6
Ending Cash Balance	$631,873	$1,481,514	$2,504,696

The projected financial statements over the

five year projected period track the financial performance.

BALANCE SHEET	Year 1	Year 2	Year 3
Total Current Assets	$11,994,982	$31,692,066	$57,667,683
Net Property Plant & Equipment	$3,801,520	$2,967,040	$2,132,560
Total Assets	$15,796,502	$34,659,106	$59,800,243
Total Current Liabilities	$1,469,523	$257,078	$264,198
Total Liabilities	$1,469,523	$257,078	$264,198
Total Shareholder's Equity	$14,326,979	$34,402,028	$59,536,046
Liabilities & Equity	$15,796,502	$34,659,106	$59,800,243

BALANCE SHEET	Year 4	Year 5
Total Current Assets	$89,734,576	$122,524,608
Net Property Plant & Equipment	$1,298,080	$463,600
Total Assets	$91,032,656	$122,988,208
Total Current Liabilities	$272,816	$276,641
Total Liabilities	$272,816	$276,641
Total Shareholder's Equity	$90,759,840	$122,711,567
Liabilities & Equity	$91,032,656	$122,988,208

The company carries no receivables as all wettings are pre-paid. The only major fixed asset is the company owned truck. There is no long term debt.

WATER FOR EQUITY SWAP

Income Statement	Year 1	Year 2	Year 3
Total Gross Revenue	$41,623,184	$65,114,662	$72,918,016
Direct Selling Costs	$49,142	$1,342	$2,161
Revenue after Selling Costs	$41,574,042	$65,113,321	$72,915,855
Total Water Cost	$0	$0	$0
Gross Profit	$41,574,042	$65,113,321	$72,915,855
Gen & Admin overhead	$12,362,105	$19,099,308	$20,156,552
Total Salary Expenses	$18,412,800	$18,412,800	$18,412,800
Total Oper and Ohead	$30,774,905	$37,512,108	$38,569,352
Operating Profit	$10,799,137	$27,601,212	$34,346,503
Depreciation	$834,480	$834,480	$834,480
EBIT	$9,964,657	$26,766,732	$33,512,023
Pre Tax Income	$9,964,657	$26,766,732	$33,512,023
Less Corp Taxes	$2,491,164	$6,691,683	$8,378,006
Net Income	$6,826,979	$20,075,049	$25,134,017

Income Statement	Year 4	Year 5
Total Gross Revenue	$82,264,056	$83,945,627
Direct Selling Costs	$2,728	$780
Revenue after Selling Costs	$82,261,328	$83,944,847
Total Water Cost	$0	$0
Gross Profit	$82,261,328	$83,944,847
Gen & Admin overhead	$21,382,322	$22,095,264
Total Salary Expenses	$18,412,800	$18,412,800
Total Oper and Ohead	$39,795,122	$40,508,064
Operating Profit	$42,466,206	$43,436,782
Depreciation	$834,480	$834,480
EBIT	$41,631,726	$42,602,302
Pre Tax Income	$41,631,726	$42,602,302
Less Corp Taxes	$10,407,931	$10,650,576
Net Income	$31,223,794	$31,951,727

Revenue is premised on several key operational factors.

Number of months that wetting takes place	12.00
Wettings per farm per month	2.00
MM3 of water needed per average farm per year	600
Customers per day per truck	4
Cost to Farm per wetting	$7,000
Contractor rate per 5 M3 water	$4,800
Price per M3 to well owner	$200.00
Market Penetration	3.50%
Direct selling costs as % of Total Revenues	1.00%

The primary factor is market penetration which is assumed at 3.5%. This results in the following rate of market penetration.

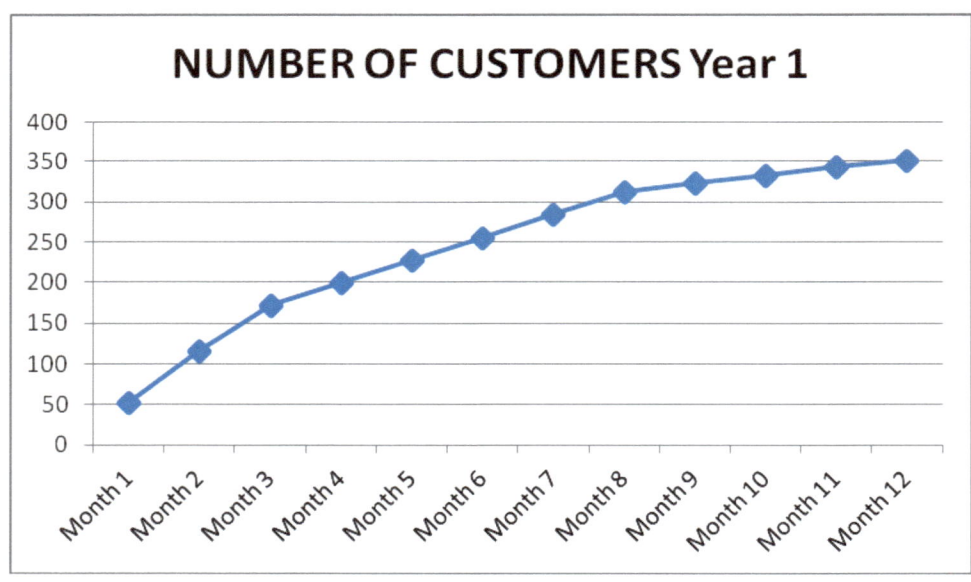

NUMBER OF CUSTOMERS

	Year 1	Year 2	Year 3	Year 4	Year 5
Month 1	53	353	363	377	390
Month 2	116	355	366	380	392
Month 3	172	357	368	383	393
Month 4	200	357	369	384	393
Month 5	228	358	370	385	393
Month 6	256	358	371	386	394
Month 7	284	359	372	387	394
Month 8	312	359	372	388	394
Month 9	323	359	372	388	394
Month 10	333	360	373	389	395
Month 11	344	360	373	389	395
Month 12	351	360	373	389	395

The operation results in the following valuation parameters.

Valuation Parameters		Year 1	Year 2	Year 3
WACC	18.0%			
EBITDA	($12,831,026)	$10,799,137	$27,601,212	$34,346,503
Discounted EBITDA	($12,831,026)	$9,151,811	$19,822,761	$20,904,342

	Year 4	Year 5
EBITDA	$10,799,137	$27,601,212
Discounted EBITDA	$9,151,811	$19,822,761
NPV	**$77,938,103**	

Valuation Parameters		Year 1	Year 2	Year 3
WACC	18.0%			
NET INCOME AFTER TAX	($12,831,026)	$6,826,979	$20,075,049	$25,134,017
Discounted NET INCOME	($12,831,026)	$5,785,575	$14,417,588	$15,297,339

	Year 4	Year 5
NET INCOME AFTER TAX	$31,223,794	$31,951,727
Discounted NET INCOME	$16,104,886	$13,966,394
NPV	**$52,740,756**	

Valuation Parameters		Year 1	Year 2	Year 3
WACC	18.0%			
Unlevered FCF		($12,831,026)	$5,141,496	$19,697,084	$25,975,617
Discounted FREE CASH FLOW		($12,831,026)	$4,357,200	**$14,146,139**	**$15,809,562**

	Year 4	Year 5
Unlevered FCF	$32,066,893	$32,790,032
Discounted FREE CASH FLOW	$16,539,747	$14,332,825
NPV	**$52,354,447**	

The weighted average cost of capital (WACC) is assumed at 18% but can be changed depending on the perspective of the promoter. Accepting the strictures of this model the net present value (NPV) is positive using the outputs of EBITDA, net income and free cash flow.

The link below is the full excel version of the financial model. Some worksheets have been protected to ensure that core formulae are not inadvertently modified. If your particular initiative requires access to protected cells contact the author at gksummers2004@yahoo.com or 876 819-8671.

If you have a print copy of the book contact the author at gksummers2004@yahoo.com for your free copy of the financial model.

Microsoft Office
Excel Worksheet

END

RESEARCH SOURCES

Upward Antony, *Towards an Ontology and Canvas for Strongly Sustainable Business Models: A Systemic Design Science Exploration*, 2013

Jamaica Observer Sunday, February 03, 2013

Daily Gleaner Tuesday May 12, 2015

The Sunday Gleaner July 19, 2015; In Focus page G6

Maps by AGAMS (Advanced GIS Analysis and Mapping Solution)

A framework for community and economic development by Rhonda Phillips and Robert H. Pittman

Triple Bottom Line Accounting: A Conceptual Expose by Atu, Omimi-Ejoor Osaretin Kingsley *ACA, FCMA, ACTI, AAT, MBA, M.Sc, PGD, DIPL.Ph.D- inview* Lecturer Department Of Accounting Igbinedion University, Okada Edo State.

The Triple Bottom Line: What Is It and How Does It Work? By Timothy F. Slaper, Ph.D.: Director of Economic Analysis, Indiana Business Research Center, Indiana University Kelley School of Business

Tanya J. Hall: Economic Research Analyst, Indiana Business Research Center, Indiana University Kelley School of Business

Theory to Practice: The Scope, Purpose and Practice of Prefeasibility Studies for Critical Resources in the Era of Sustainable Development

URAM, Vienna, June 23-27, 2014

Market imperfections, opportunity and sustainable entrepreneurship by Boyd Cohen, Monika I. Winn University of Victoria, Faculty of Business, P.O. Box 1700 STN CSC, Victoria, BC, Canada, V8W2Y2

Received 1 December 2003; received in revised form 1 March 2004; accepted 1 December 2004

Sustainable Entrepreneurship: A Convergent Process Model by Frank Martin Belz1 and Julia Katharina Binder Technische Universität München, TUM School of Management, Freising, Bavaria Germany, Technische Universität München, Freising, Germany

United Nations University Policy Brief number 1, 2011 Innovation and Entrepreneurship in Developing Countries

Cannibals with forks: The triple bottom line of 21st century business by John Elkington 1997

Paper: Capital Budgeting and Corporate Responsibility Mr. Balraj Kistow Lecturer – Finance and International Business & Doctoral (DBA) Candidate Arthur Lok Jack Graduate School of Business, UWI

Dr. Ron Sookram Lecturer – Corporate Responsibility Arthur Lok Jack Graduate School of Business, UWI

Sustainability Accounting and the triple Bottom Line by Andrew James Carrick 1 December 2012

It consists of three Ps: profit, people and planet

Nov 17th 2009 | Online extra

STATIN FARM CENSUS - 2007

Gordon Keith Summers (Keith) is a native of Mandeville in the parish of Manchester, Jamaica. He attended high school at St. George's College in Kingston and Fordham University in New York where he attained a BS in Finance and an MBA degree. The substance of his experience has been in Banking and Corporate Finance where he has functioned as both employee and consultant.

It was late in his career that he was introduced to community economic development at an intensive level. It has been a driving element in his professional pursuits ever since.

www.ingramcontent.com/pod-product-compliance
Lightning Source LLC
Chambersburg PA
CBHW040925180526
45159CB00002BA/619